Coconut Oil Benefits

2nd EDITION

Successful Guide to Coconut Oil Benefits, Cures, Uses, and Remedies!

Glowing Skin

Shinning Hair

Fast Weight Loss

Healthy Living

Written By: Julie Gordon

Table of Contents

Introduction

Coconut oil is a substance that has been used across the globe for some time now, but its originated use was in the southeastern Asian continent. Scrolls have been found dating back four thousand years that show that coconut oil was used, even back then, as a medicinal substance, and as a dietary staple. It comes from the fruit of the coconut palm. Most often, the oil is derived from a pressing method, and this was the method our ancestors used in order to extract the coconut oil from the dried kernels, also known as copra. This practice is still used today, but the old ways of extracting coconut oil are more costly than extracting it using a machine.

Just as it was used during the ancient times, coconut oil is used today as a medicinal supplement, has cosmetic purposes, and is even used as a dietary supplement. It has antibacterial, antifungal, and antiviral properties in order to protect the body from harm and help it heal much faster than normal. Taking coconut oil on a daily basis and using it topically can greatly reduce your risk of infection and illness. It is also an excellent anti-inflammatory for those who suffer from a fever or chronic stress that may lead to heart disease.

During the forties, coconut oil seemed to lose favor because of its high triglyceride content; however, coconut oil contains medium chain triglycerides, which are not harmful to the heart or arteries in any way. In fact, it does contain the long-chain triglycerides, which are substantially harmful to cardiovascular health.

Therefore, if you fear that coconut oil is not good for your heart, rest assured that it is actually the opposite! Read further for more information on how you canuse this tasty, nourishing oil for medicinal, cosmetic, and dietary purposes.

Chapter One:
The History of Coconut Oil

Before you begin to use coconut oil, you should know some of the historyof its uses as this history will shed light on just how purposeful this one product of the coconut is.

Four thousand years ago, the Ayurveda medicine texts were written in Sanskrit, and they outlined the health benefits of coconut oil. Those who lived in the Southeast Asian countries, such as the Philippines and Indonesia, referred to the coconut oil as the tree of life due to its source of plant-based fats. It was and has been used as an energy-dense food that provides both highly valued nutrition and medicinal properties.

Interestingly enough, during World War II, soldiers would poke an intravenous tube into a coconut and use the fluids as sterile hydration for those who were injured or sick. Due to its unique composition of electrolytes, essential amino acids, natural sugars, and antibacterial properties, the coconut water was very similar to extracellular and intracellular fluids.

In the past century, coconut oil has become a preferred source of plant fats for food manufacturers in the North Americas due to its texture, taste, and stability. In the forties, seed and vegetable oils from cottonseeds, corn, and soybeans began to replace the coconut oil due to its diet-heart hypothesis. This hypothesis suggested saturated fat contributes to heart disease and its development, and coconut oil is high in saturated fats. Unfortunately, this new development made coconut oil disappear from the American diet for many decades.

Even though it may have disappeared from the dietary end of the usage, coconut oil remained prominent in the healthcare industry. It turns out coconut oil is a natural source of medium-chant triglycerides, which are used to treat critically ill patients. Therefore, coconut oil was an excellent choice for patients who had a compromised fat digestion issue or sensitive gastrointestinal tracts.

The medium-chain triglycerides were extracted from the coconut oil and used to treat gastrointestinal disorders and promote ketosis in patients were who attempting to follow a ketogenic diet in order to treat refractory epilepsy.

As like many other oils, coconut oil is one hundred percent fat, yet the type of fat is unique. Dieticians are very much aware of the high content of saturated fat in coconut oil as it makes up more than eighty-five percent of its fatty acids. But one of the more interesting facts about coconut oil is that sixty-five percent of the fats are present in the form of medium-chain fatty acids, as opposed to long-chain fatty acids. MCF acids have fourteen carbons in length, and they don't have to break down into a single fatty acid in order for the body to absorb it. MCT's find their way to the liver via a portal vein and bypass the carnitine transport system for mitochondrial entry.

Now, around forty-nine percent of the medium-chain fatty acids in coconut oil are lauric acid, and the rest are made up of many different types of acid. This fatty acid profile creates a stable substance that is protected against oxidation and heat damage. Therefore, it's optimal for cooking because it's not easily broken down by heat.

Lauric acid is also known to be an antimicrobial substance, and when it infiltrates the membranes of the lipid-coated bacteria, fungi, protozoa, or viruses, it can destabilize them and cause them to disintegrate. This kills the microbes.

However, the process can only happen if there is a sufficient amount of blood concentrations of lauric acid.

Now that the general public is educated about these different properties of coconut oil, they are beginning to realize that it's an excellent addition to the diet, as well as cosmetic and medicinal routines. So let's take a look at some of the different types of coconut oil so that you know which one you are purchasing and which ones you will need for medicinal, cosmetic, and dietary purposes.

Chapter Two:
Types of Coconut Oil

Not all coconut oil is created equal and this section shall discern the different types of coconut oil that you can find in the market. However, there are some things that are generally the same for coconut oil. Almost all coconut oil is edible (with exception of hydrogenated coconut oil). The typical make up of coconut oil is approximately 90% saturated fat, 6% monounsaturated fat and 3% of polyunsaturated fat.

This make means that coconut oil is very stable in heat, and can be heated to temperatures that are quite high without there being any negative effect to its make-up. In addition to this, coconut oil has the added advantage of having a long shelf life.

There are several varieties of coconut oil on the market at this time and these include pure, organic, refined, organic virgin, extra virgin, and virgin. One of the key ways that these oils will vary from each other is in the way that they have been refined. Refining basically refers to the way the oil is extracted from the coconut, before it can actually be used as an oil.

The coconut oil that has been refined the least, and is most like fresh coconut is the virgin oil.

Pure Coconut Oil

Pure coconut oil is extracted from the copra or dried coconut kernels, and this most widely used and known type of coconut oil on the market (Copra also refers to dried coconut that has been removed from the shell but remains inedible until it has been processed further to produce coconut oil;). This coconut oil is extracted using compression of the dried coconut kernels in a mill, and it is crude and unrefined when it gets to the buyer. Pure coconut oil is very versatile as it can be used for medicinal, cosmetic, or edible purpose. It even has industrial uses!

Refined Coconut Oil

This coconut oil is a refined, bleached, and deodorized product. It is produced by mechanically and chemically refining the crude coconut oil. They make it thin, odorless, colorless, and without any proteins suspended in the product. They are often copra based prior to being refined. RBD which stand for refined, bleached and deodorized, is a term that is often used to describe refined coconut oil.

The term bleaching may fill one with trepidation to try this oil, especially if it is understood as a process of adding harmful chemicals to the oil. Fortunately, it does not refer to this at all. Rather, it involves a special bleaching clay which is used for the purpose of filtering. The filter is supposed to take out any impurities that are in the copra, before it is turned into oil.

This type of coconut oil has a bland flavor, and when it comes to smell, there is not very much of it. As some people may be concerned about the flavor of coconut oil affecting their meals, consuming refined oil will take care of that concern. It is also ideal for all sorts of cooking because it has a high smoking point.

Should you opt to purchase refined coconut oil, you will find that it readily available and usually cheaper than virgin oil. In addition, it has a multitude of uses. In addition to being suitable for cooking and meals, it can also be used to create soaps, bath oils and moisturizers for the body.

The process of refining this oil does have a disadvantage, and that is that some of the nutrients are stripped away. Nonetheless, it is still very close in nutritional value to virgin oil. Not all refined coconut oils are the same. Here is a breakdown of the four refined oils that you are likely to come across at a market or grocery store.

Coconut Oil

Usually, there is some description that is given with an oil to differentiate it from other similar types. However, if you find an oil that is simple labeled as coconut oil, without any further description, then it is likely to be an RBD oil. You need to be careful when purchasing this oil, particularly if you want to ingest it. Go through the label carefully, and ensure that there are no harmful solvents that could have been used during the refining process.

Expeller-pressed Coconut Oil

In the United States, most of the coconut oil is produced by entirely automated machines. However, there are tropical countries who refine their oil in a completely different way, and they use a process known as mechanical "physical refining" from the copra. Whereas fully automated extraction may require the use of chemicals like hexane in the refining process, coconut oil that is refined physically does not have these chemicals. Therefore, some consider it to be cleaner.

Liquid Coconut Oil

When you place coconut oil in the fridge, it is likely to change its composition from being a liquid to something a little more solid. However, coconut oil manufacturers have created coconut oil that does not behave in this way, and that is what is referred to as Liquid Coconut Oil. This type of coconut oil is referred to as 'fractionated coconut oil'. It is oil that contains no lauric acid.

Liquid coconut oil has a lower melting point than the ordinary coconut oil.

Hydrogenated Coconut Oil

If you are seeking an edible coconut oil, this is the one type that you should avoid completely. This oil is not edible, and can actually cause harm within the body. It contains dangerous Trans fats, which come about once a minimal portion of the unsaturated fatty acids have been hydrogenated. The effect of this is that the coconut oil will remain more solid at higher temperatures.

Virgin Coconut Oil

This coconut oil is actually made from the milk from the coconut meat and not from the copra. The processes used to create this coconut oil are through centrifugal separation and fermentation. There is very little to no heat used in the extraction of this oil, and when it's produced this way, it tastes and smells the best. It's also riddled with antioxidants and medium chain fatty acids. Virgin coconut oil is one of the best varieties of coconut oil and can be used for medicinal, cosmetic, and dietary uses.

If it the delicious flavor of coconut that you are seeking, then you will find that in virgin coconut oil. Some of these oils have very intense flavors, particularly if there was some heat applied during the extraction process. The scent of coconut is also present in this oil

An oil is determined to be virgin based on the way that it has been produced. One of the ways involves pressing out the oil from a dried coconut. By using this method, producing coconut oil en masse becomes quite simple. Once all the oil has been squeezed out, the coconut flesh can be turned into desiccated coconut and used for another purpose.

Most of the virgin oil is also derived through what is referred to as a wet milling process. This involves the oil being extracted from coconut meat that is fresh, meaning it has not been dried. The process begins by expressing the coconut milk out of the coconut flesh. The oil is then separated from the liquid.

Organic Virgin Coconut Oil

While this form of coconut oil is the rarest form, it is perhaps one of the best forms of coconut oil. It uses the same process as virgin coconut oil, but the oil is produced in an organic way from organic coconut kernels.

Extra Virgin Coconut Oil

This is perhaps one of the most controversial of all coconut oils as there isn't an actual virginity scale for coconut oil and no one knows what extra virgin coconut oil really is, it seems. There are no government regulations when it comes to the virginity; thus, it's best to stay away from this type of coconut oil as it doesn't really make any sense to call it extra virgin.

Organic Coconut Oil

Organic coconut oil is much like regular coconut oil, except it's been extracted from coconuts that are harvested from palms that are raised on organic manure and are not treated with insecticides or synthetic fertilizers. The production also does not involve a chemical extraction process, and only involves pressing. These organic coconut oils are used in organic cosmetics, soaps, dietary supplements, and much more.

Carrier Oil

Coconut oil as a carrier oil is very efficient as it absorbs readily through the skin, allowing other oils and nutrients to follow it. It's also excellent because it doesn't go rancid, and keeps the other oils and nutrients added to it from going rancid, as well. It has an anti-fungal and anti-microbial property that keeps it from growing bacteria or fungus in order for it to go bad.

Coconut Oil Quality Ratings

With all these different options that are available, you may be wondering which would be the best coconut oil for your to purchase and use. It all depends on what you want to use the coconut oil for, and your budget, although whatever you choose, you are almost definitly going to enjoy a host of benefits. Here is a basic rating scale that will help you decide on what would be the best quality option. The rating scale starts from 0 being the least favourable, going up to 10 being the most favourable.

Hydrogenated Coconut Oil

This coconut oil has a rating of 0 and should be avoided as much as possible, especially for consumption. When used in cooking it could become toxic and damage the body in one way or another. In addition, there are better options out there for anyone wanting to enjoy the cosmetic benefits of coconut oil.

Liquid Coconut Oil

With a rating of 1, this oil is better than hydrogenated, although that is not saying too much. It is missing lauric acid, a component of coconut oil that is improtant for it to have some nutritional value. It also has a low smoking point, and has been refined. It is a possible option if you are on a tight budget, but do not expect any miracle benefits.

Refined Solvent Extract Coconut Oil

Coconut oil can be refiend in several ways, and this refers to coconut oil which has been refined using chemicals. It receives a rating of 4. It is useful and affordable, although its main disadvantage is that it may contain some chemical residue which could be both unappealing and harmful.

Refined Physical Coconut Oil

This coconut oil has a rating of 6, and it is a good coconut oil for general use. It can be used for cooking as well as a range of other uses in the home and on the body.

Fresh Pressed Virgin Coconut Oil

Virgin coconut oil is extracted from the coconut meat in various ways, and when it is fresh pressed it receives a rating of 8. This rating indicates that the oil is very good, and can work with a range of uses. If you use it for cooking though, you will have some of that delicious coconut flavour in your meals.

Wet Mill No Heat Virgin Coconut Oil

This coconut oil receives a rating of 9 which means that it is excellent. It is rich in nutrients, and can be used in any fashion. It has added health benefits within the body when consumed.

Wet Mill Fermentation Heated Virgin Coconut Oil

This is the only coconut oil that has a rating of 10, and that is because it is the best. Since it has been created with the use of some heat, it is high in antioxidants, making it better for consumption as it can work in more areas within the body. This is the oil that you should strive to get if you want to experience the full benefits that you can enjoy by trying out coconut oil.

Extracting Coconut Oil

Cold pressing or expeller pressing are the best options for extracting coconut oil as it does not damage the quality of the oil. Cold pressing uses the dried coconut kernels and either uses a machine or manual pressing method. The machine method is done using electricity or a diesel-engine powered mill, and most of the cold pressed coconut oil is processed this way. Manual pressing is through a literal person pressing the oil from the kernels, and it's very expensive this way. It also tastes a lot better and has an amazing fragrance compared to other coconut oils.

The second main way to obtain coconut oil is boiling the fresh coconut milk, which destroys a lot of the health benefits of the coconut oil. It is preferable to not use coconut oil obtained this way.

Purchasing Coconut Oil

Before you go ahead and purchase coconut oil, you should figure out which purposes you will be using it for. For instance, if you are going to cook with coconut oil, you want to purchase refined coconut oil. If you are using coconut oil to lose weight, you will want virgin. If you want the coconut oil for cosmetic reasons, you may want to use pure, virgin, or refined coconut oil.

If you are going to use coconut oil for a therapeutic or hygienic purpose, you want to use refined coconut oil as it is the cleanest.

When you're purchasing coconut oil, you can most likely find the variety you need from a local grocery store or a health food store. You can also find coconut oil online, but be very careful who you purchase it from and what their reviews are before you buy. You don't want to get ripped off! Just because some coconut oil has an exorbitant price, does not mean that it is of the best quality. In addition, only purchase as much as you need because while it may not go rancid, it may lose some of its nutritional properties after a very long storage time.

Coconut oil also varies by color, especially at different temperatures. When it is a solid, it should be pure white in color. In liquid form, it should be completely colorless. If it is available in any other shades, or has some discoloration, then it could mean that the oil has been contaminated. Other colors are also an indication of inferior quality, which could mean that you do not receive the results that you require.

When you are purchasing coconut oil, also try and take in the smell of the oil. If it has a strong coconut scent, it is an indication that it is a virgin oil or is unrefined. However, this scent should in no way be overpowering. Should the oil also smell smokey or as if it has been roasted, it means that it was exposed to a lot of heat when it was being created, and this may affect the amount of nutrients that have been retained within the oil. Refined oil will have no odor and will also taste neutral.

Finally, storing coconut oil is very simple. You can store it at room temperature, but beware that it will melt above seventy-six degrees Fahrenheit. You can also keep it in the refrigerator if you'd like to keep it a solid.

Now that you know which type of coconut oil to purchase and how to store it, let's look at some of the different uses for coconut oil.

Chapter Three:
The Medicinal Uses of Coconut Oil

There are hundreds of different uses for coconut oil when it comes to medicinal uses, but in this chapter I will focus on some of the most popular and helpful uses for health. Consuming coconut oil medicinally involves taking a capsule or consuming the oil without any other foods in order to absorb the oil quickly. Some of the different health benefits will go along with diet benefits.

Let's start with the most common use of coconut oil for medicinal purposes today, weight loss.

Weight Loss

It seems counterproductive to ingest more fat in order to lose fat, but coconut oil contains 2.6% fewer calories in a gram than most other fats regularly used in cooking. While that may not seem like a significant difference, it actually makes a large impact over time.

In a study published in the American journal of Clinical Nutrition in March of 2008, forty-nine overweight men and women were put onto a calorie-restricted diet that consisted of eighteen hundred kcal for men and fifteen hundred kcal for women. They either consume a daily dose of MCT oil derived from coconut oil or olive oil. Eighteen grams total for the women and twenty-four grams total for the men were consumed on a daily basis. This went on for sixteen weeks. Both study groups lost weight, but weight loss was greater in those who were in the MCT oil group. They lost around seven pounds while the olive oil group only lost three.

The reason for this is that the MCT's that are found in coconut have an interesting effect on the body, and that is the fact they help the body expend energy. They do this much more effectively than the calories that you will find from longer chain fats. An increase in energy means that more calories are burnt, and the final effect of this is better weight loss. Over the long term, consuming coconut oil would be an excellent way to lose weight, or at the very least, to maintain and balance the weight that you currently have.

This information is backed up by scientists who discovered that it was the unique structure of the triglyceride fats in the MCT oil that made it easier to burn, harder to store, and increased thermogenesis. Thus, it made weight loss easier for those who consumed it because their bodies were functioning in order to lose weight. Those who participated in the trials also found that they were less hungry and had stable energy levels.

Coconut oil also has the ability to suppress one's appetite, meaning that you eat less which will eventually result in weight loss. This is suspected to be due to the method in which the coconut oil is metabolized within the body, particularly its existing fatty acids. Anyone who is seeking long term weight loss would consider this to be an excellent benefit.

Therefore, coconut oil is a great tool for weight loss, and consuming up to thirty milliliters or two tablespoons of it a day via cooking and straight ingestion is safe and effective.

Cardiovascular Disease

While most dietitians and physicians are not yet comfortable recommending that their patients consume coconut oil because it has a high saturated fat content, take into consideration a study that was conducted over the course of twenty-three years. In March of 2010, this study was published in the American Journal of Clinical Nutrition. There were three hundred and fifty thousand participants who were followed over the course of twenty-three years, and their diets were tracked. The study showed there is no correlation between the consumption of saturated fat and the risk of cardiovascular disease and stroke.

If you're a fan of double-blind studies, this one ought to impress. Forty middle-aged Brazilian women who suffered from abdominal obesity were given two tablespoons of soybean or coconut oil every day for twelve weeks. When the trial was over, both groups have shown weight loss, but the coconut oil group had a remarkable decrease in waist circumference. The soybean oil group's LDL cholesterol increased significantly and their HDL levels decreased. Their cardiovascular profile had worsened while the coconut oil group's had gotten better.

Coconut oil is a natural anti-inflammatory, and chronic stress causes chronic inflammation, which will lead to a stroke and cardiovascular disease. Consuming coconut oil on a daily basis reduces that risk significantly by decreasing the inflammation in the arteries and veins, as well as around the rest of the body.

Neurological Conditions

Alzheimer's disease is actually referred to as type 3 diabetes due to its association with the decline in glucose metabolism in the brain. In fact, the inability for the brain to metabolize glucose leads to many other conditions, such as Parkinson's disease, malignant brain cancer, and many others. Studies had shown that when Alzheimer's patients consume MCT oil, their glucose metabolism in the brain improved.

Another disease that can be improved with coconut oil consumption is Type 2 diabetes. Coconut oil is able to significantly improve the body's insulin secretion as well as the way that the body utilizes blood glucose. This helps alleviate some of the symptoms of diabetes, which in some cases can be life threatening.

Dieticians are suggesting that eating a higher fat and lower carbohydrate diet may keep those who are at risk from developing neurological conditions, and it will improve those who already suffer from them.

Healing Wounds

Coconut oil has been used to heal wounds for thousands of years. There are three important processes the coconut oil goes through as it heals the wound. It accelerates the rebuilding of new tissue, improves the enzyme activity to get rid of dead tissue, and stimulate the collagen linking in the tissue in order to bind it together quicker. Coconut oil can be used on any type of wound, as long as it is not a life-threatening wound that may need stitches or further care.

Coconut oil is also excellent for anyone who wants to prevent any scarring after they have received a cut some sort. In addition to the benefits that have been mentioned earlier, coconut oil is also able to help any new blood vessels form much faster, and this in turn enables the body to produce healthy skin which has no scars.

Anti-Inflammatory

Coconut oil is an excellent anti-inflammatory and has great fever-reducing properties. Take two tablespoons of coconut oil in the morning if you're feeling unwell, and you'll start to feel better as if you had taken any other NSAID pain reliever.

Inflammatory diseases may affect the digestive tract and in this sense damage the colon. Taking in some coconut oil can help, especially as it is a dietary fat source. With its antioxidant and anti-inflammatory effects, it is able to offer protection.

Anti-Fungal Properties

Spread some coconut oil on your toe fungus or ingest it in order to rid your body of Candida. Coconut oil is versatile in the way it can be used to treat fungus, and can be used internally or topically. Candida is a fungus that can grow in the body and is also known as yeast. The overgrowth of it can cause symptoms similar to those of irritable bowel syndrome.

It can also be used on all sorts of rashes and blemishes which may be fungal in nature, and as it conditions the skin, the overall healing result will improve both the look and the feel of skin. To ingest it for use within the body, you can add it to your beverages, or simple eat it with a spoon. It can also be incorporated into dishes that you are cooking.

Testosterone Booster

Coconut oil has also been found to reduce the oxidative stress in the testes of rats, which resulted in higher levels of testosterone. So while it's not testosterone in itself, it will help men's bodies create more testosterone the natural way.

This is because for the body to create testosterone, it needs to have some saturated fat. Coconut oil is 90% saturated fat, and that is what gives it such a great advantage.

Energy Booster

Coconut oil can be used as an effective energy booster. You do not need to depend on high sugar calorie drinks for a burst of energy if you have coconut oil at hand. All you need to do is mix some of the coconut oil with chia seeds, and consume. Make sure you take this energy booster in the morning, or you may be in for a long night wide awake.

Improved Blood Lipids

Coconut oil has been proven over and over again in numerous studies to improve the LDL levels and the HDL levels in patients. It creates a healthy ratio.

Reducing Seizures

Coconut oil has fatty acids which once they are in the body are converted into Ketones. People who are on ketogenic diets are able to treat various diseases, one of which is epilepsy, especially in children. A ketogenic diet works by inducing ketosis, which is the state the body goes into when it has been deprived of carbohydrates but pumped up full of fats. The more fats there are in the body, the more ketones are present.

MCT's that are found in coconut oil travel to the liver, and once they are there, are converted into ketone bodies. They can then create a state of induced ketosis, while still allowing the person to consume carbohydrates.

Bone Health

When oxidative stress is reduced in the body, the body is able to produce healthier, stronger bones; thus, it helps prevent osteoporosis.

Sunscreen

Coconut oil will block out UV rays by thirty percent, but it does not block out the UVB rays, which are beneficial to your skin and health.

As you can see, coconut oil is an excellent medicinal additive to your daily regime as it's an anti-fungal, anti-bacterial, anti-inflammatory, and anti-microbial substance. So how can you get the best out of coconut oil and use it in a cosmetic sense while also using it in a medical sense?

Read on to find out!

Chapter Four:
Cosmetic Uses for Coconut Oil

There are many different cosmetic uses for coconut oil for both men and women! Here, I'm going to give you a number of different uses you can start using today.

Makeup Remover

Coconut oil is an excellent makeup remover! You can put it directly on your skin and an oil cleanser or you can allow it to sit on your skin using a cotton pad. Your makeup will melt away, and not even the strongest water resistant mascara is going to be able to resist it.

Breath Freshener

Because it has antifungal and antibacterial properties, coconut oil is actually an excellent breath freshener. Just gargle with it for twenty minutes to clear away the germs in your mouth, which will lead to fresher breath and whiter teeth.

Lice Remedy

Combine a tablespoon of apple cider vinegar and a tablespoon of coconut oil, and then apply it to your head and allow it to sit for twenty-four hours. Then brush your hair with a fine-toothed comb and shampoo as normal. The lice will be gone!

Body Lotion

If you're someone who likes to make their own body lotions, coconut oil is an amazing choice! You can use it to make any type of body moisturizer with a few drops of essential oil, or mix it up alone by using a mixer to beat it into a fluff.

Cuticle Oil

Do you have dull nails with cracked cuticles? Then try placing some coconut oil balm at the base of your nails. This will also help that manicure last a little longer!

Makeup Brush Cleaner

You should clean your makeup brushes at least monthly, so use a cleanser that is two tablespoons of antibacterial soap and one tablespoon of coconut oil in order to strip the makeup off the brushes and kill off any lingering bacteria.

Lip Balm

If you suffer from chapped, dry lips in the winter time, just add a dab of coconut oil to your lips and feel the soothing effect. It'll also help repair them quicker because it will draw moisture to them and heal them faster.

Stretch-Mark Cream

If you suffer from stretch marks during or after pregnancy, use some coconut oil in order to ease the appearance of marks. You can also use this on scars in order to lighten them a little. It may not get them to go away, but they will fade.

Undereye Cream

Coconut oil will get rid of those dark marks and the fine lines under your skin, as well as ease puffiness due to its anti-inflammatory properties. Just apply a dab underneath the eyes before bed and be amazed by the effects in the morning!

Body Scrub

Mix just half a cup of coconut oil with some coarse salt or sugar in order to make exfoliate. The moisturizing oil will stay on your skin even though the course grains have melted away, creating a barrier against bacteria and keeping your skin soft.

Frizz

Do you suffer from flyaways during the summer months or humid weather? Then use a dime-sized amount of coconut oil on your hands and massage it into the midshaft and ends of your hair. It will also give your hair an extra shine!

Massage Oil

Nothing beats having a massage after a bad day or using it as a sexy way to be together as a couple, and an all-natural alternative to those chemical laden massage oils sold in stores is coconut oil. Just warm it in the microwave, ten seconds at a time until it's at the desired temperature, and then add some drops of essential oils to make a soothing massage mix.

Whitening Toothpaste

Are you looking for an organic, make it yourself alternative? Then try using some coconut oil with a little baking soda in order to whiten your smile and freshen your breath!

Shaving Cream

Shaving cream does not have to have lather in order for it to work properly, and coconut oil is an excellent shaving cream when you use it in the shower. It also helps to moisturize your legs and keep razor burn from being an irritant to turning into an infection.

Dandruff Treatment

Most know that dandruff comes from not only a dry scalp, but also from a bacteria on the scalp. Use some coconut oil and massage it into the root every night in order to add moisture to the hair and stimulate hair growth, as well as get rid of those pesky bacteria.

Body Oil

Use some coconut oil after a bath or shower and slather it on your wet skin. Then towel dry and be amazed at how soft your skin is and how much it glows!

Itch Relief

No one likes bug bites and itching wounds, so add a little coconut oil to your regime to get rid of that itch. Its antibacterial properties will help the bug bites and wound heal faster.

Conditioner

Use some coconut oil in your hair as a preconditioner before you get into the shower or add a little to your shampoo in order to make a soothing, moisturizing wash experience. Or even add a little after you shampoo as an all-natural conditioner.

If you want to wake up with super soft hair, you can leave coconut oil in your hair before you go to bed and it will act like a leave in conditioner.

Night Cream

Place some coconut oil on your face in order to get rid of those fine lines and wrinkles. The antioxidants are amazing!

Deodorant

You can make a DIY deodorant at home using coconut oil! Just mix some coconut oil with a little cornstarch, baking soda, and a scented oil for all day protection again odor and moisture.

Fixing Dry Hands

When working in the home, especially when hands are exposed to harsh chemicals while washing dishes or handling household chemicals, they can get dry and unsightly. In some cases, they could even begin to feel hard. Coconut Oil works as an excellent moisturizer and gets soaked into the skin quickly, allowing for welcome relieve for parched hands.

Highlighter

If you take the time to read the labels on your make up, you will find that many brands use coconut oil as a core ingredient. You can do so too, without having to purchase expensive brands. Take some coconut oil on top of your make up, apply a small amount, especially above the cheekbones. It is a natural highlighter and will perk even the most tired looking skin.

Chapter Five:
Dietary Uses for Coconut Oil

From this moment onwards, you should consider using coconut oil in all your foods. If is an excellent substitute for any other oil that you may have been using, and its health benefits means that it is actually good for you, and can improve your overall health.

If you are used to butter or margarine, especially when baking or creating desserts, you can immediately substitute them with coconut oil. In all your frying, you can do the same thing, as coconut oil has a high smoking point and compliments the flavors of many foods.

You can even use coconut oil to create mayonnaise so that you can have a super healthy salad. Unlike other oils, you can consume coconut oil with a spoon as its flavor is sweet and not too strong. What you need to do is refrigerate it and when it is solid, dig in.

There are many different uses of coconut oil as a dietary supplement because sometimes healing of the outer body has to come from the inside. Here, I'm going to give you some reason as to why you should consume coconut oil on a daily basis.

Hair Health

Not only can you use coconut oil as a shampoo, conditioner, and treatment for lice and dandruff, you can consume coconut oil in order to repair damaged hair and help your scalp grow health, new hair. Consuming coconut oil on a daily basis helps restore the proteins in your hair follicles, which produce the oils that make your hair shiny and healthy.

When you regularly consume or massage your hair on a daily basis with coconut oil, you are giving it the proteins and other nutrients it needs in order to be beautiful.

Skin

Coconut oil has been used topically in order to treat psoriasis, eczema, dermatitis, and severe dry skin problems, but when you consume it on a daily basis; you will help your skin heal from the inside out! Due to its antioxidant properties, it has been known to prevent premature aging and degenerative disease, so it's an excellent skin care regime that you can add to breakfast, dinner, or lunch!

Immunity

Coconut oil is an excellent supplement to strengthen your immune system because it has antimicrobial lipids, lauric acid, caprylic acid, and capric acid. These all have antiviral, antifungal, and antibacterial properties. The body uses the lauric acid to make monolaurin, which helps protect the body from diseases such as the influenza virus, herpes, HIV, and cytomegalovirus. It also helps in getting rid of harmful bacteria in the system such as listeria monocytogenes and harmful protozoa such as giardia.

Digestion

When used as cooking oil or consumed on a daily basis as a supplement, coconut oil helps keep your digestive system regular. Thus, it's an excellent supplement for those who have irritable bowel syndrome and constipation issues. It is also a mild laxative when consumed in higher doses so it can help for those days when you're feeling particularly bloated. Coconut oil also helps you absorb nutrients better through the intestines as the nutrients attach to the coconut oil and are carried through the intestinal walls with the oil.

Candida

Systemic Candidiasis is a disease that is caused by the overgrowth of yeast in the stomach. It is present in every person's stomach, yet some seem to have an uncontrolled amount of it in their systems. It's growth is actually controlled by other bacteria in the digestive system, but sometimes that bacteria can be damaged or even killed off by antibiotics. This leads to an imbalance of candida in the system.

Symptoms of this unfortunate disease can include an infection of the urinary tract, bladder, genitals, stomach, intestines, nose, ear, throat, skin, and internal organs. These can lead to itchy, dry skin, patching and peeling skin, digestive complications, and even problems with nails and hair.

The illness is particularly common in both America and Europe, most likely due to the moist, cold climate and the improper storage and preparation of food. Alcohol, bread, and cheese are all contributors to the overgrowth of Candida in the system with the beneficial bacteria are not present. However, the fatty acids are found in coconut oil are actually great at counteracting the effects of Candida.

One of the medium chain fatty acids, Capric acid, is also an antiviral, antimicrobial, and antifungal. In the body, it will react with enzymes that are secreted by bacteria, and convert those enzymes into an antimicrobial agent. The use of coconut oil will become effective in killing off the Candida and curing the disease.

Therefore, coconut oil has been shown to cure and prevent Candida and provides relief from the inflammation caused by the overgrowth of the yeast. It keeps the skin from cracking and peeling, and it's a gradual change, which helps those suffering from Candida avoid the Herxheimer Reactions. The Herxheimer Reactions are the symptoms that come along with the body rejecting the toxins that are created by the elimination of the Candida fungi.

Healing and Infections

When coconut oil is applied to an outer area of infection, it protects the infected area from air, dust, bacteria, viruses, and fungi. It also helps speed up the healing process of bruises.

As aforementioned, the antifungal, antibacterial, and antiviral properties of coconut oil help fight off conditions such as the measles, influenza virus, herpes, hepatitis, SARS, ulcers, urinary tract infections, throat infections, gonorrhea, and pneumonia. It is also effective against athlete's foot, diaper rash, and thrush.

Using coconut oil internally can protect against many different diseases and illnesses. Just consume two tablespoons a day of coconut oil and keep the doctor away!

Other Uses

Coconut oil has been recommended for many different ailments, some of which are mentioned in this section. Be aware that it has only been shown to mildly help some of these conditions, but it does help.

- **Liver:** Because there are MCT's and fatty acids in coconut oil, it helps prevent liver disease because the substances are converted easily into energy once they get to the liver. They reduce the workload on the liver and prevent the accumulation of fat.

- **Kidney:** Coconut oil has been shown to prevent gall bladder and kidney related disease, as well as help dissolve kidney stones.

- **Pancreatitis:** Due to its ability to be absorbed easily, coconut oil has been shown to be useful in treating this ailment.

- **Stress:** Consuming coconut oil on a daily basis helps you alleviate mental fatigue and stress.

- **Bones:** Coconut oil improves your body's ability to absorb minerals and nutrients it needs in order to develop and heal bones. Therefore, it is especially useful for women who are middle-aged in order to avoid osteoporosis.

- **Dental Care:** Coconut oil will help you avoid tooth decay because it will keep your gums healthy, and it will help your body absorb calcium in order to build and maintain strong, healthy teeth.

- **HIV and Cancer:** Coconut oil has actually been shown to play a role in reducing the viral susceptibility for cancer and HIV. It reduces the viral load of those who already have been infected with the HIV virus in order to help keep their immune systems healthy.

- **Alzheimer's disease:** As aforementioned, there have been studies that show that coconut oil consumption leads to the mitochondria in the brain being able to absorb glucose sent to it in order to thrive and heal. There is hope that coconut oil may help prevent or at least alleviate the symptoms of Alzheimer's patients.

Chapter Six:
Coconut Oil for Babies and Children

There are many baby products that are available on the market, and the more aware that the consumer becomes, the more one begins to realize how dangerous they can be when the baby uses them. Many people are opting for organic products which do not contain the harmful ingredients that can affect a baby's skin, leading to dryness, eczema and a host of other skin conditions.

While choosing products that are organic, you should look even further at the exact ingredients that are within these products. The gentler they are, the better because baby's skin tends to be very sensitive. This chapter contains the different ways that you can used coconut oil for a baby.

Increase Milk Supply and Nutrients

The life of your baby begins at conception, and it is from this point that you should begin to consume foods that will nurture your child and give them the best chance at life. Coconut oil provides nutrients to the unborn baby that aid in their growth and overall development.

In addition, a lactating mother can take some coconut oil each day, as it has been proven to help boost milk production. If you have nipples that become dry and begin to crack, rubbing a little coconut oil in them will be soothing, and will also speed up their healing making it easier for you to continue breastfeeding.

Cleaning Newborn

When you bring your newborn home, they will pass meconium the first few times they go expel their waste. Meconium is a thick, gluey, greenish black substance. Due to it being so sticky, it can be quite a challenge to clean off. A little bit of coconut placed on a coconut swab will make the job much easier for you.

Rash Prevention

You need to be 100% sure of what you are putting on your baby's skin, particularly in the sensitive genital area. Coconut oil is an excellent oil to use when creating cream to prevent diaper rash. It is very unlikely to cause any allergies, and it offers good protection. At the same time, it has properties that help make the skin more supple, moisturized and smooth. This means that in addition to offering protection of the skin, it helps the skin to look softer and shiny.

Baby Products

You should use coconut oil to create a range of skin and cosmetic products that your baby will use. Coconut oil can be used to create baby powder, baby lotion, baby oil and other skin care products. Coconut oil is all natural and us hypoallergenic.

Healing

Many babies fall victim to cradle cap, a harmless yet unsightly skin condition that often affects the head and sometimes spreads around the body. Coconut oil can be used on cradle cap, to loosen the scales that are on the head and safely result in smooth skin on the scalp.

Weight Gain

Having a premature baby can be a terrifying and heart wrenching experience. One of the things that a parent would be worried about is how they can get their little one to put on weight. Some research has discovered that by massaging a premature newborn with coconut oil on a daily basis, weight gain as well as overall growth improve significantly. Plus, there is the fact that this oil will help to moisturize the skin, and ensure it remains supple and elastic.

Treating Diarrhea

This applies to toddlers as well as young children as a benefit of using coconut oil. It is known to reduce the length that a little one could suffer from diarrhea if incorporated in small doses into the child's diet.

Cradle Cap

Young babies less than three months old are often afflicted with cradle cap. These crusty flakes that appear on the scalp are painless, though they are unsightly. By soaking your baby's head with coconut oil, you will find that they quickly slide off without have any effect on the child's wellbeing.

Skin Moisturizer

Most babies love bath time, and it can have even more added benefit if you incorporate some coconut oil into it. By adding a few drops into your baby's bath, you are able to instantly moisturize the baby's skin, keeping it soft and supple.

Chicken Pox Relief

Chicken Pox can leave your child in discomfort, scratching everywhere and leaving scars. Taking a little coconut oil all day, both internally and applying it topically will have several positive effects. First, it will relieve any itching that your little one experiences and second, it will reduce any inflammation around the 'pox' sites. In addition, it will help lessen the duration that your child is afflicted.

Chapter Seven:
Using Coconut Oil in the Home

The previous chapters have looked extensively at how coconut oil can be great for you, especially when it comes to both your internal and external body. In addition, coconut can be used around the home to offer excellent protection to certain items, or even in some cases, as a lubricant.

Here are some practical ways that you can use coconut oil around the home: -

Soften Leather

If you own a leather couch, it is likely that you occasionally face a challenge keeping it smooth and avoiding it cracking over a period of time. Coconut oil can fix these issues for you. It is recommended to use coconut oil on shiny leather. The coconut that is used will soften the leather, making it more comfortable to sit on, and the coconut oil also acts as a conditioner that prevents cracking and drying out of the leather.

Seasoning Pans

When you have purchased a cast iron pan you need to season it well before you use it. Coconut oil is the ideal oil to use for this process. All you need to do is make sure that you have coated the pan very well with coconut oil. After this, you should place the pan in a cool oven, and then turn on the heat to 300 degrees. Close the oven door and leave the pan in there. After around 45 minutes, you should switch off the oven. You can then begin to use the cast iron pan once it has adequately cooled off.

Remove Stains

Should you have some stains that are on your carpets or any upholstery, then you can use coconut oil to create a solution that will quickly and efficiently get rid of them. All you need to do is mix together one part of coconut oil with one part of baking soda and place a little bit of this mixture on the stain. Once you have left it to site for a short while, perhaps five minutes, you can simply wipe it away and you will notice the stain vanish.

Polishing Furniture

Rather than purchasing an expensive polish for your wood furniture, you should use a coconut oil mixture. This mixture should include ¼ cup of coconut oil in liquid form, 4 tablespoon of distilled white vinegar and 2 teaspoons of lemon juice. Combine all of these items in a spray bottle by shaking them together well. Then you should spray this onto your wooden furniture, and use a clean cloth to wipe and polish. This will protect and clean the wood, and give it an amazing, long lasting shine.

Repelling Insects

If you have an issue with creepy crawlies and flying insects, you can use coconut oil to create a natural insect repellent that is hypoallergenic and that will not cause you any discomfort. By mixing coconut oil with peppermint essential oil and applying to your skin, insects will literally do what they can to get away from you and you will finally be able to enjoy that warm cup of coffee on your patio in peace.

Should you have been the unfortunate victim of an enthusiastic mosquito such that your body is covered in itchy mosquito bites, coconut oil can offer you some much needed relief. All you need to do is day some coconut oil on the bite and the itching will stop. It also offers the added benefit of healing without leaving behind a nasty scar. As coconut oil has properties in it that are antibacterial, the risk of the mosquito bite becoming infected significantly reduce.

Get Rid of Chewing Gum

Little girls and boys will often get themselves into a little scrap, and having chewing gum stuck in the hair is one such scrap. You can easily loosen the grip of a stubborn piece of chewing gum by applying some coconut oil to the chewing gum. Let it sit there for a few minutes and you will be surprised that the chewing gum will easily slide off the hair.

Clean Shower Scum

Over time, you will begin to notice that there is some scum that gets stuck between the tiles in your shower, and this can turn dark and unsightly. It can also be quite a challenge to remove. However, by putting a little bit of coconut oil on a rag, you can wait until your shower floor is dry and gently rub away at the scum. This should easily take it right off the tiles.

Polishing Bronze

The beauty in bronze lies in bringing out that fantastic color, and using coconut oil as a polish will serve two purposes. The first is that it will bring out the color well, and in some cases even make the color deeper and richer. In addition, it will also help to keep your bronze items clean.

Rust Remover

It is highly possible that at the back of your kitchen drawer is a pair of scissors or a set of knives that have been abandoned because they have become rusty. Coconut oil can be used to get them back to their previous shape. All that is required is to cover them with coconut oil on their blades, and then leave them to sit with the coconut oil for approximately an hour. After that you should rinse them with hot water and you will notice the rust disappear.

Take Labels of Jars

Would you like to reuse a fancy glass jar but have not so far due to a stubborn label that will not come off? Coconut oil is the solution that you need. What you should do is completely cover the label with a layer of coconut oil and allow it to soak in for around three minutes. You should easily be able to slide the label off, or to wipe it off. Should there still be a little stickiness left behind on the bottle, a soft towel with a drop or two of oil will get rid of it.

Lubricate Small Motors

The kitchen contains numerous appliances, some of which operate with motors. For motors to move effectively, they should have some lubrication. All you need to do is add a drop or two of coconut oil and your appliances will be good to go. Do not go overboard though. Anything more and you could cause some malfunctions.

Zipper Control

If you have a bag or a pair of jeans that have a sticky zipper that will not move up and down its teeth adequately, adding a little bit of coconut oil to it will have it moving smoothly again. Once you add the oil, pull it up and down a few times to make sure the oil really goes into the teeth well. Avoid getting the oil on the fabric, especially if want to avoid any possible staining.

Polish your Bathroom Silver

All the faucets and taps in your bathroom could shine brightly if they are polished with a little coconut oil. Simple rub the oil directly onto the metal, and allow it to sit there for a short while. Next, use a soft cloth to gently polish and enjoy the bright shine.

Keep Dust at Bay

When you have some coconut oil wiped onto your surfaces, you will aid in repelling dust and when you need to clean up, it will be much easier to do so.

Chapter Eight:
Coconut Oil for Pets

Dogs and Cats are domesticated pets that often become significant members of the family's that they live in. It is no wonder that dogs are described to be man's best friend, because indeed, they offer companionship, protection and loyalty. Taking care of a pet in the best way possible is the priority of many pet owners, and coconut oil can help improve a pet's wellbeing immensely.

This chapter touches on some of the benefits that even your pet can enjoy is they have coconut oil incorporated into their meals.

Elevates Metabolism

Just like human beings, dogs can suffer from deficiencies or issues with their diets that lead to them having problems with metabolism. These problems can lead to the dog putting on weight and being unable to shed it. Rather than go for something drastic or surgical, coconut oil should be consumed by the dog.

Coconut oil will work in much the same way in dogs, as it would in humans. In humans, the MCT's once metabolized are able to offer an immediate supply of energy which aids in weight loss and enhances physical stamina. In dogs, MCT from the coconut oil works on the thyroid and balances it, which helps with weight loss for overweight dogs, and also increases the energy levels of dogs that may be a little lazy. Coconut oil is able to do this gently, leading to more sustainable and healthy results in the long run.

Protects from Illnesses

Coconut oil offers excellent benefits to the immune systems of dogs and cats, strengthening them and helping protect from illnesses. This is because coconut contains a significant amount of powerful antiviral, antibacterial and antifungal agents. In addition, coconut oil is able to help regulate as well as balance the levels of insulin within the dog. Dogs are able to get diabetes, just like humans, and taking coconut oil is a good preventive measure against this chronic illness.

Other health problems that older large dogs often suffer from include arthritis, or issues with the ligaments around their joints. Coconut oil offers relief from these possible issues.

Speeds Up Healing

If you have a dog or cat with a cut or some infection, you may find that coconut oil can considerably help to speed up healing. When seeking medical care for your pet, they may be prescribed some medication or given an injection. This is turn could lead to a reaction that makes the problem worse than it had been originally.

Coconut oil is a natural product, and when used in the right form will reduce any allergic reactions that the dog or cat may have. One of the infections that coconut oil can treat excellently is any yeast infection. In addition to treating them, it is also ideal to use as a preventative measure for these infections.

Dogs and cats cannot safely use the same disinfectants that human beings use. Coconut oil is an effective disinfectant for their wounds, it is not painful to apply and it helps to promote rapid healing. Coconut oil can actually speed up the healing of all sorts of cuts, as well as any bites or stings, and even on small open wounds.

Excellent for Coat Maintenance

Different dogs have different sensitivities, particularly when it comes down to their coats and maintenance of the same. Coconut oil can help to clear skin conditions that may cause hair loss and itching, and generally lead to the discomfort of your pet. Therefore, if your dog or cat has eczema, or is allergic to fleas you can rub in coconut oil on the affected areas. This also helps with dogs that have contact dermatitis and skin which is itchy.

The health of your dog's skin is also important, as this can affect how much the dog sheds and their overall look. Coconut oil protects your dog's skin, resulting in a better looking and feeling dog.

When your dog goes running around in bushes, digging up holes or kicking up dirt in the garden, they are likely to pick up and maintain a heavy, rather unpleasant dog odor. Their coats are also likely to be a mess, and if long haired, you may have knots to contend with. Coconut oil helps coats become glossy and sleek, making maintenance much easier. In addition, that doggy odor can be quickly eliminated or deodorized with a little pat down containing olive oil.

Improves Digestion

Dogs and cats are known for eating all sorts of different foods, but that does not mean that all these foods agree with their systems all the time. In many cases, it is necessary to help your pet's digestive system to perform better, as they are also prone to having running stomachs or constipation.

Coconut oil helps to improve the digestion of pets as it increases the nutrient absorption within the animal's system. For pets who are afflicted with digestive disorders, coconut oil will help in healing areas of inflammation as well as addressing the cause of the illness.

Just like in human beings, dogs are prone to bad breath, particularly if their digestion is not up to par. Coconut oil will reduce the bad breath that your dog may have, and in some cases, may eliminate it completely.

After cats have cleaned themselves thoroughly, they may have to contend with stubborn hairballs causing blockage in their throats. Coconut oil helps these come up much easier, which in turn prevents the coughing and gagging that is often accompanied with spitting up hairballs.

After reading all these benefits, you are likely to want to immediately start incorporating coconut oil into your dog's meals. In order to experience these benefits in the best possible way, you need to be careful how much you are putting in their food. The recommended dosage according to leading veterinarians is ¼ teaspoon for every ten pounds of body weight, given twice daily.

Chapter Nine:
The Myths of Coconut Oil

Coconut oil has been used for centuries by certain Asian cultures, and it has brought forth many health benefits to the people who have used it. It is only within the last decade that it has started to become more popular in the United States, and for that reason, consumers are still trying to figure out how to deal with coconut oil. Some wonder whether it is safe to cook with, others, whether it can treat skin conditions and so on.

However, there are some myths that have cropped up about the benefits of coconut oil, and some of them are misleading. This section shall address some of these myths, to offer clarity and answer burning questions.

Myth 1

Virgin Coconut Oil is better for you than Refined Coconut Oil

To start, this myth has no basis due to one simple factor – all coconut oil is good for you. However, as the world is obsessed with understanding fats and what they do to our bodies, the saturated fats in refined coconut oil are giving it this negative approach.

In coconut oil, it is the medium chain fatty acids that do a significant amount of good within the body, and they are still intact in refined coconut oil.

Myth 2

In the long run, the saturated fat from coconut oil will cause heart disease.

We have been educated over the past few decades about the dangers of saturated fats in the system, and how they clog up the arteries and lead to high cholesterol, cardiovascular issues and in the worst case, death as a result of a heart attack. No wonder there are people who have voiced concern over the use of coconut oil in the long term, particularly because evidence has revealed that coconut oil contains saturated fats.

Research has been carried out on the native populations who have been consuming coconut oil for centuries, and it has been revealed that this consumption has not resulted in heart disease of any nature, and therefore, cannot be linked to cardiovascular issues.

Myth 3

Coconut Oil is not for me. I could be allergic.

It is possible for someone to imaging that they are allergic to coconut oil, particularly if they are allergic to other nut oils. Oils like peanut oil and sesame oil can cause serious allergies, which if unmanaged, could even result in death. A coconut is not a nut in this sense, so one does not need to worry about being susceptible to nut type allergies.

An understanding of what causes allergies is necessary to dispel the myth that one could be allergic to coconut oil. Allergies are usually a result of the body being unable to properly digest certain proteins that are found in food. Although the coconut meat contains these proteins, they are absent in coconut oil. If one faces some problems with the digestion of coconut oil, it is more likely to be as a result of not being able to digest fats of all sorts, rather than an allergy to coconut oil.

Myth 4

Coconut oil should not be used by diabetics because it is sweet

This myth is untrue and misleading. Although coconut oil does have a pleasant flavor, it is now sweet and does not contain any glucose within it. If anything, coconut oil is good for any diabetic, as it has healing properties. In addition, it helps with the secretion of insulin from the pancreas, controlling diabetes. It can be used as a preventive measure for those who are at risk or suspect that they will contract the disease.

Myth 5

Coconut oil has a short shelf life as it has moisture

One should not confuse the moisture that you find from a coconut with what you would expect to find in the oil. Coconut oil is amongst the most stable oils that you can find, and therefore, this myth does not hold any water. It is able to last for years longer than a range of other oils. In fact, it would probably take several years before it even began to show a hint of becoming rancid.

Myth 6

Coconut Oil is a passing fad and will soon be replaced by something else

This is not true, as coconut oil has been used for centuries in tropical countries. It is only recently that it has been introduced to the western world, and that is why there are so many questions being raised about its properties and its uses. Once thing is for sure though, it has a significant number of positive benefits.

Coconut oil is not a passing fad or a super food. It is an ingredient that is readily available, has always been, and will probably continue to be available for the considerable future.

Myth 7

Coconut oil is good for you as it boosts your immunity

Here is a myth that is actually true. The fatty acids that are found within coconut oil can be used to heal viruses within the body. In addition, the antibacterial and antifungal properties of coconut oil go a long way to boosting the system. Within the body, coconut oil can use its antimicrobial properties to sooth parasites like those that cause Candida, and this can result in better digestion or a reduction in bloating.

Myth 8

Coconut oil is excellent for skin care

This is very true. It has so many positive properties going for it. To start with, when it is applied on the skin it gets absorbed easily and does not have a greasy effect at all. It can be used by people with all skin types, and if you have little cuts and bruises on your skin, it will help to heal them.

Should you have skin that is covered in stretch marks or you have some stubborn wrinkles on your face, coconut oil can work wonders in smoothing them out.

Myth 9

Coconut oil will help me get skinny

If you have been suffering from weight control issues, coconut oil could be your saving grace. This myth is true. Coconut oil, if consumed on a daily basis, can increase the number of calories that one burns in a day. In addition, it also helps one overcome their cravings and protects the body from insulin resistance.

Myth 10

Coconut oil is the miracle answer for all afflictions

There is no doubt that coconut oil has a considerable number of advantages. It works in all parts of the body, helping with weight loss, boosting immunity and even improving the functionality of the brain. Research has shown that it is not a miracle answer in entirety, because there still exist some products that compete with it and produce better results. For example, it has not been recommended as a suitable substitute to extra virgin olive oil, which is an unsaturated oil.

Myth 11

Coconut oil is a teeth whitener

This myth has some truth in it. Coconut oil can significantly improve dental health by getting rid of bacteria. In addition, swirling it in the mouth for a duration of time, a process known as oil pulling, can really help with whitening the teeth.

Myth 12

Coconut oil is the best oil you can consume

This is a myth, although coconut oil does have significant benefits. To begin with, when compare with butter and other Trans fats, coconut oil us exceptionally good for you and would make a suitable substitute. It is cholesterol free.

However, the fact that is has a large amount of saturated fat means that is viewed as not being as good as vegetable oils. It is better than hydrogenated Trans fats. It has been suggested that those looking for health benefits should opt for other oils like canola or olive oil.

Although coconut oil has been available for centuries, particularly in Asian cultures, researchers in America are still, trying to figure out all the benefits that it has, and whether it is worth consuming in the long run. Therefore, there is still some research that can be done to further dispel or agree with these myths. In addition, more research needs to be done on human subjects for better results, as it has been found that a large amount of the research that has been done was conducted on animals.

For now, it is recommended that coconut oil should be consumed, although moderation is key until more research proves that it is one of the best options that a person can find.

Chapter Ten:
Coconut Oil Products

Now that you know of all the benefits that you can enjoy with coconut oil, this section contains some products that you can make on your own so that you can experience all these products for yourself. The best thing about making your own products is you know all the ingredients that are within them, and you can make sure that everything is of the highest quality. If you suffer from allergies, the methods here will help you create products that are hypoallergenic, anti-fungal and all round good for you.

Coconut Oil Shampoo Bars

Your hair can benefit greatly from coconut oil use, as it will get moisturized and a natural shine. Here is a recipe which will help strengthen any type of hair. These shampoo bars are suitable for all hair types, and will not strip away at any of your hairs natural oils.

Ingredients

300 ml coconut oil

300 ml olive oil

300 ml palm oil

350 ml distilled water

175 ml castor oil

150 ml lye

30 ml essential oils of your choice

Method

1. As you will be handling lye, you need to make sure that you are wearing thick rubber gloves as well as some large protective eyewear. Make sure to go outdoors for this part of the mixing.

2. Place the water in a large glass bowl. Slowly add the lye to the water. Remember that the mixture will become quite hot. Stir with a wooden spoon until it is well mixed and then put it aside to cool.

3. In a separate pot, add all the oils and slowly warm them on low heat. When they have melted well and are warm (not hot), again, slowly add in the lye mixture to the pot.

4. Using a wooden spoon, mix thoroughly until it is the consistency of thick custard.

5. Add in your essential oils.

6. Now, pour the mixture into a mold and cover it with a cardboard box. The mixture will remain in this state for 24 hours.

7. Once 24 hours are up, you can remove the soap from the mold and cut it into bars if you wish. Now, your bars need to cure in an area with good ventilation. This will take approximately six weeks. Once the curing process is complete, you are ready to begin using your shampoo bar.

Coconut Lotion Bars

These are bars that you can easily rub on your skin to moisturize it. They make excellent gifts, and as they are in the form of bars, you do not need to worry about spillage in the way you package them. You can also use attractive moulds to create the shapes that desire.

This recipe is basic, and you are free to add any essential oils you desire to change the scent of them.

Ingredients

    1 cup of coconut oil

    1 cup of beeswax

    1 cup of shea butter

    1 teaspoon of essential oil of your choice

Method

1. Begin by putting the coconut oil, beeswax and shea butter in a large glass mason jar. Place this jar into a saucepan of boiling water. Make sure none of the water falls into your mixture. You should leave the jar in the water until all its components have melted. Make sure that you constantly stir them so that they are also smooth and well blended. You may have the saucepan going on low heat.

2. Take your mixture off the heat, and mix in your essential oils. Make sure to stir them in gently, until you feel that they have been thoroughly incorporated.

3. Pour your mixture into moulds of your choice. Allow the mixture to cool and once it is completely cool and solidified, you can take it out of the moulds.

4. This recipe will produce a total of 10-12 lotion bars.

Coconut Oil Deodorant

You need to be careful about what you put on your body, and a deodorant made from all natural ingredients can be of great benefit – especially if it protects you from some terrible body odor. Here is a recipe that you can try on your own.

Ingredients

½ cup coconut oil

½ cup baking soda

1/3 cup shea butter

1 teaspoon essential oil of your choice

Method

1. Get a mason jar and place within it the shea butter and the coconut oil. Melt them together in a saucepan that is half full of steaming hot water.

2. Once the mixture has melted, add in the baking soda. Make sure that you have mixed everything together well.

3. While it is still liquid, add in your choice of essential oil.

4. Pour the mixture into a deodorant stick containers. If you are unable to find a new one, you can easily recycle one that you have completed using in the past.

Coconut Oil Sun Screen

No matter where you live, it is important that you always have your sunscreen with you, and that your entire family uses it too. As it is a product that you will use often, it is essential that it be completely natural, and do good for your skin. It would be a shame to develop a cancerous condition, simple because you were using a sunscreen that increased your risk.

Here is a recipe you can use to prepare a perfect sunscreen using coconut oil.

Ingredients

1 cup olive oil

½ cup coconut oil

½ cup beeswax

1 teaspoon vanilla essential oil

4 tablespoons zinc oxide

Method

1. Get a glass mason jar and put in it the olive oil, coconut oil, beeswax and vanilla essential oil. Mix these all together well.

2. Put a saucepan on the stove and fill it up halfway with water. Bring the water to the boil.

3. Cover the Mason jar loosely and place in the hot water once it has boiled. Stir the mixture or shake it up to ensure that all the ingredients within it have melted.

4. Once they are melted completely, add in the zinc oxide and make sure to stir it well.

5. Cool it, and it is immediately ready for use. One batch will last you a good six months (shelf life).

Coconut Oil Laundry Detergent

Purchasing natural laundry detergents that are not laden with chemicals can be expensive, and therefore, it makes sense to create your own laundry detergent. You also have the benefit of incorporating all the properties of coconut oil into it. Here is the method you will use.

Ingredients

1 liter coconut oil

175 ml lye

350 ml water

30 ml essential oil (rose or lavender are good)

1 cup borax

1 cup washing soda

Method

1. Your first step will be to make some laundry soap. Go outdoors and make sure you have a large glass bowl, you are wearing plastic gloves and using a wooden

spoon with a long handle. In this bowl, mix together the lye and the water. Start with the water in the bowl and then add the lye. Stir slowly and consistently. Please be careful because after a short while, the mixture will become very hot. It will go through a transition, starting off as cloudy and ending up clear. Once it is clear, you should leave it to rest for 10 minutes.

2. While it is resting, take a large saucepan and gently melt your coconut oil. Take it off the heat. Now, add in the lye mixture slowly, and avoid splashing. Stir it as you do so. Once it is all in, stir it vigorously until it is about as thick as a pudding.

3. Return to the heat and allow if to cook on very low heat. This should take at most 40 minutes. You will know it is ready once it appears to be a little translucent and does not have any puddles of oil in the centre. In your fingers, it should feel waxy.

4. Once the mixture has cooled, you can add in some essential oils. Then, spoon the mixture into a mold of your choice and place it in the refrigerator to cool. Now you have created some laundry soap. This will be a core ingredient for your laundry detergent.

5. Take one bar of your laundry soap, and grate it so that it forms small particles which will be able to dissolve quickly.

6. Mix this together with your borax and washing soda.

7. Your detergent is now ready, and you can use 2 tablespoons for each load, whether you are using a machine or hand washing.

The first section detailed some coconut oil products that are ideal for use around the home. You can also create coconut oil products which you can eat, and these will help with building up your body. Here are a few recipes that you can refer to.

Coconut Oil Smoothie

Ingredients

1/3 cup coconut oil

1 ½ cups coconut milk

½ teaspoon vanilla extract

2 egg yolks

1 cup ice

Cocoa powder/banana/cinnamon – or any other flavor you like

1 tablespoon gelatin

Method

In a blender, combine all the ingredients and give this a good blitzing. Serve with a side of chocolate chip and oatmeal cookies.

Chocolate Chip and Oatmeal Cookies

Ingredients

2 cups whole-wheat flour

1 cup rolled oats

1 cup walnuts

1 cup dark chocolate chips

2/3 cup maple syrup

2/3 cup virgin coconut oil

2 teaspoons vanilla extract

A little water

Method

1. Preheat the oven to 350 F degrees. Take a baking tray and grease with coconut oil.

2. In a large bowl, combine the flour, oats, chocolate chips and walnuts. Make sure that they are mixed together well.

3. In another bowl, combine the coconut oil, maple syrup and a little water (a tablespoon or two will suffice).

4. Create a well in the dry mixture. Pour in the wet mixture and mix well.

5. Take the dough and create small balls. These should be flattened and placed on the baking tray.

6. Bake for 20 minutes. When ready, cool on a wire rack.

You could also prepare some fresh herbs for use when cooking, and preserve them in coconut oil. This would add a whole new dimension of flavor to all your meals. Here is how to do this.

Herbs Frozen in Coconut Oil

Ingredients

Some fresh basil, rosemary and dill (or any other herb which you may prefer)

Coconut oil

Method

1. Begin by preparing your herbs. You will need to wash them thoroughly and then strip them from their stems. After this, chop them up into small piece one at a time. You want to make sure that they are all finely chopped. You can mix some of them together if you want to create a herb mix.

2. Next, take an ice cube tray and fill each compartment within the tray with approximately a tablespoon of herbs.

3. In a small pan, melt the coconut oil. Do not make it too hot, you only need it to be in liquid form.

4. Place one tablespoon of coconut oil above each compartment with the herbs and when you have filled up all the compartments, place in the freezer.

5. Once the herb cubes have frozen, pop them out of the ice cube tray and place them in little bags within your freezer.

6. All you need to do is pop them into a soup or stew when you need to use them.

The family pet also benefits greatly from coconut oil. Here is a recipe for some dog biscuits that your pooch will love.

Yummy Coconut Oil Dog Bickies

Ingredients

1 large sweet potato. Boiled and cooled.

1/3 cup coconut flour

1/3 cup coconut oil

1 egg

1 tablespoon water

¼ cup of gelatin powder

Method

1. Preheat the oven to 350 F degrees.

2. In a large bowl, combine the sweet potato, coconut flour, coconut oil, egg, water and gelatin powder. Make sure to mix well until you form a nice and soft, firm dough.

3. Divide the dough into balls around an inch each.

4. Using your hands, flatten each ball.

5. Place on a baking tray that has been greased with coconut oil and bake for approximately 18 minutes. These will be ready when the edges are a little brown.

6. Take out of the oven and cool before taking off the baking tray.

Giving your dog one of these each day will help immensely to boost their health and wellbeing.

FAQ's

Why is coconut oil a solid?

Most want to know why coconut oil is solid when we usually see oils as a liquid. Coconut oil is only solid below seventy-six degrees Fahrenheit, so if you want it to melt, simply heat it up just a little on the stovetop. You can do this by using a double boiler method or even popping it into the microwave for ten seconds.

How do you use coconut oil?

Another question is how do you use coconut oil? Well, if you want to use it for topical reasons, just melt it and keep it in a bottle that is in the sun or sit the bottle in warm water for a few moments. If you want to use it internally, then just replace the vegetable oil or butter with coconut oil in the recipe. You do not have to melt it for this purpose.

Can you use coconut oil for cooking?

Yes, you can use coconut oil for any type of cooking as long as you are not going above three hundred and fifty degrees

Fahrenheit. Above this temperature, it may begin to lose some of its nutritional value, but that's all. The burn rate for coconut oil is actually pretty high, so you don't have to worry about it catching on fire as you deep fry with it or sauté with it.

Animal fats are not good for your cardiovascular system, especially as they lead to higher cholesterol levels which are damaging to health. When baking, you can substitute butter for coconut oil. You are guaranteed to get a lovely consistency, and also an excellent surprising flavor to your baked goodies.

What if I don't like the taste of coconut oil?

If you just don't like the taste of coconut oil while you're cooking, try using it in something like baking in order to incorporate it into your diet. If you become nauseous or feel sick after you ingest coconut oil, do not continue to ingest it! As with any other food item, you may be allergic to it.

How much coconut oil should I consume in a day?

The quantity that you need to consume will vary according to your age. However, an adult should aim to consume around 3 ½ tablespoons of coconut oil in a day. If you have not been taking in any coconut oil at all, start with a tablespoon a day and work your way up to the daily recommended amount. This will give your body time to get used to the coconut oil.

Do I need to keep my coconut oil in the fridge?

Coconut oil does not need to be kept in the fridge. This is because it is mainly saturated and therefore is stable and unlikely to go rancid. However, you can choose to store your coconut oil away from direct silent. A cool dark place would be best.

Is coconut oil affected by the weather?

When it is very warm, it is likely that your coconut oil will be in liquid form. However, if the temperature drops to below 24 degrees, than it will change form and become a solid. This does not in any way affect the benefits that you can enjoy from coconut oil, neither does it affect the nutrients that are within the oil.

What are the calories in coconut oil?

For those who are conscious about their weight, they can enjoy coconut oil without too much guild. It actually has been proven to contain a fewer calories that some other oils, and especially butter. Every tablespoon of coconut oil has approximately 117 calories.

How exactly can I begin consuming coconut oil?

You can start off by using coconut oil for all your cooking. You can also use it as a replacement for milk in your tea or coffee. When having breakfast, adding a spoonful to oatmeal and cereal will add flavor and texture. If you are consuming virgin coconut oil that has a stronger coconut flavor, try spreading it onto a cracker and enjoy a distinct coconut flavor.

If you use coconut oil as a substitute in baking, a 1:1 ratio is acceptable.

How is coconut oil different from olive oil?

As both of these oils are hailed to have health benefits, it may be confusing trying to decide which one would be the best for you. Coconut oil is a saturated fat, and it is quite stable. Olive oil is a monounsaturated fat, and it is much more sensitive to the elements. In fact, olive oil can easily oxidize due to prolonged exposure to heat or light.

Coconut oil will not change its nutritional structure under these conditions, and is not likely to end up being oxidized. Both of these oils offer health benefits from essential fatty acids. However, olive oil is best taken in raw, and coconut oil can be eaten raw, though will have nutritional effects if taken in dishes which have been cooked.

What are the benefits of coconut oil in a nutshell?

There are very many benefits of coconut oil as you have noted throughout this book. In a nutshell, coconut oil is excellent for cosmetic purposes, especially skin care and health care. Within the body, it boosts the immune system and aids in digestion. It is also able to regulate the metabolism. When it comes to diseases, high blood pressure and diabetes benefit from consistent coconut oil usage. Some more advantages can be seen in dental use, as coconut oil can help to whiten the teeth as well as improve the strength of the bone. If you have weight issues and want to lose some, coconut oil will help you get closer to meeting your weight loss goal. Coconut oil is antimicrobial, antifungal, antibacterial and also an antioxidant.

Conclusion

As you can see, there are so many amazing benefits to coconut oil when it's used both externally and internally! You can prevent that mid-winter flu or cold virus and you can heal your dry, damaged skin. You can even use it during the summer time in order to prevent sunburn! Whatever your needs, coconut oil most likely has a curative property that will help. With its antibacterial, antifungal, antiviral, and anti-inflammatory properties, it can sooth even the nastiest of infections.

Remember that while coconut oil is a great addition to anyone's health regimen, you should still seek advice from a doctor or dietician if your symptoms do not improve. In addition, do not continue the use of coconut oil if you suffer intestinal upset, such as gas, bloating, or diarrhea for a prolonged period of time. If you suffer from a Candida infection, then these symptoms may be signs of the Herxheimer Reactions, so be sure to have yourself tested for this illness if you suffer from gastrointestinal upset while taking coconut oil.

Always be sure to obtain coconut oil from a reputable source and avoid the extra-virgin coconut oil as there really is no such thing! Whether you choose to cook with it, you want to create a cosmetic product, or you simply want to use it on your body, you should always have a little bit of coconut oil at hand. Where else can you find a product that has more benefits than you can keep track of?

I hope you enjoyed the information you found in this book and found it to be helpful. If so, please leave a review at your online eBook retailer's website.

Thank you for reading!

BONUS

3 chapters of:

Pilates

Get the Body You Always Wanted, Right Now

Table of Contents

Chapter 1:
The need for body trimming

None of us can deny the pressures on our souls because of these fast moving life patterns. All day long we move from one place to another, for working deadlines, household chores and special agreements. This has made the human life more liable towards robotic routines. Every rising sun is having some different and variant challenge. Many people owe this extensive development and progress of mankind in the field of technology and research. As more and more aspects are being conquered, the challenges for humans are also becoming gigantic. So in this tiresome war of survival, the human beings have nearly forgotten their existence and the need for taking care of one's self.

Apart from various needs like the physiological and the need for accomplishment, there have are innumerable reasons which can be listed for making the human posture fit and trim.

The tiresome routines

As discussed in the introductory notes, human life is no less than a challenge. In this venture of financial struggle many of us have become ignorant for their individualistic needs. Spending hours and hours sitting on our workstations, in a need to earn more and to get prominent position in one's corporate and social circle, we have left our self far away. Other than physical fatigue, all this tiresome challenge has posed a number of questions for the quality of life. While planning our lives, we should account for a balanced approach, an approach which can aid us in meeting the both ends. One major thing which needs to be accounted for is the dependency of this entire struggle on human health. So while on our way to challenging work life, we should also keep an eye on the need for keeping our body slim and trim.

The decreased immunity level

As all pictures having two side of analysis, the technology outburst has also given birth to a number of major aftermaths pertaining to human life. All these points are interconnected. The demanding routine of work has made individuals less concerned towards their body needs. As a result the dependency over processed and easy to eat food has increased to a horrible level. All the artificial food and processed diet patterns has made the human body internally weak, so much so that the munity level against the infections and bacterial attacks has reduced to an alarming level.

Reliance on technology big cut to physical activity

Yet another aftermath of this technology dependent human world has been observed in the shape of reduced physical activity. We have become surrounded by machines, robots and digital assistants. Form mobile phone to large space rockets all the inventions of technology has drastically altered the human routine. The increased dependency on machines has led to extremely low levels of physical activities. So the human body has become addict of no physical output. All work is done through workstations, with just a few clicks. From shopping to planning everything is mechanized form ordering to online delivery. All this has put human far from physical activity and more inclined towards obesity and health issues.

Overweight denotes social humiliation

Connecting all these major points ne major consequence is the increased trend of obesity and being overweight. The story does not end here. In fact it is the commencement of a new quandary. Because of having a detracted body, many of us have to encounter blunt remarks and humiliating statements. It is a severe trauma for the individual suffering from it, as he has a sturdy routine, and is not equipped to spend any of his time for his body trimming. The situation become even worse if re affected individual is a female. Female being highly possessive about body shape and beauty become extremely fatigued about this matter, the social mortification faced by being overweight leads towards the mental and emotional disturbances. So the need for body trimming has heightened greatly.

Chapter 2:
The Emergence of Pilates- Setting Miraculous Standards for Human World

Pilates is a term used for an exclusive classification of strengthening, stabilizing and stretching exercises, introduced about ninety years ago by Joseph H. Pilates, who was basically a German born. He was a physical culturist. The history of his upbringing strongly connotes his interest n the field of physical arts, as his mother was a naturopath and his father worked for long as a gymnast. His father won a number if pries and distinction in this filed. Being brought up in such an environment, Pilates naturally had the tendency to get interested in physical arts and exercises. He learned and practiced varying categories of exercise including yoga, both Eastern trends as well as the Western forms of exercise.

Earlier in his youth, he was skillful in a number of physical training regimes, which were practiced at that time in Germany. All this summed up for his inspiration for developing the idea of Pilates. These were the time traced back to late ninetieth century when the physical culture was taking a turn and the use of exercises as a preventive as well as a curative technique, was gaining momentum. One f the result of these changed trends was the use of apparatuses. An additional and chief whirling point in his career was the war time. At that time he got trapped in Britain because of war. During that time medical gymnastics emerged as a popular trend. Joseph Pilates also started instructing corrective exercise.

The theme line of Pilates as a fitness instrument is that the powerhouse of human body is the center of the human body. So this technique is exclusively focuses on the postural muscles, to regain a perfect posture. The apparatus used in different sessions, the Allegro Reformer, uses straps, springs, and a stirring carriage to provide for a variety of exercises and to create spatial and body awareness. Pilates is a scheme for attaining the body awareness. Having a firm belief in and having the determination to get results with Pilate's scheme will revolutionize your entire life, the mode of your feeling your own appearance will change altogether

Return to Life through Contrology

Joseph H. Pilates spent a major portion of his life in United States a and made major developments upon his research work there, Therefore United States became the major hub for the progress and popularity of this technique. It is largely being followed in the United States

Although the technique has become renowned all over the world as "Pilates" because of the unprecedented contribution of its inventor, yet the original term coined by the pioneer was Contrology, from the combination of control and logia (being of Greek origin)

In his book Joseph Pilates proposed that this scheme of exercise is basically an art of highly controlled and calculate movements, which, when properly administrated, will have a feeling of a workout, rather than some imposed kind of therapy. owed to constant practicing Pilates retains the ability to aid in getting flexibility, control, strength, develops control and endurance in the entire body and posture. It entails a prominence to breathing, alignment, coordination, and development of a strapping underline powerhouse and balance. This scheme of exercise brings out for different exercises to be adapted in a variant range of toughness, from commencement to complex or to any other level. The exercise pattern may also alter or vary depending on the personalized goals of practitioner and the choice of instructors.

Pilates had a strong belief that mental strength and physical health are highly and critically dependant o one another.

The mechanical aspects of "Pilates

Joseph Pilates being the inventor of this technique was not only a gymnast. he was also a scientist as well as a, mechanical genius This aided him o accompany his method by a set of useful equipments which he denoted as "apparatus" .The Apparatus acted as an aid to help pick up the pace or the entire process of body alignment, strengthening, stretching, and increased core strength. The best-known and most popular piece today, Reformer, was in the beginning designated as the Universal Reformer, rightly designated for reforming the body universally. As more and more progress HAS Underwent in the flied of Pilates, there has developed a full array of accessories and equipments. This includes the Pedi-Pole, Wunda Chair, Cadillac, High "Electric" Chair, Ladder Barrel and Spine Corrector.

Publications of Joseph Pilates:

- Your Health: A Corrective System of Exercising (1934)

- Return to Life Through Contrology (1945)

Modern Pilates embraces both the traditional approach of Pilates, as well as the modern additions in the scheme. The classical approach to Pilates is based on the original and unedited work of Joseph Pilates, the legend; whereas the current versions are based on slight alterations and modifications, made mostly by first generation students. But most of the people are of the view that this mixture of new and old has largely benefited the field and it has expanded the scope of Pilates from being a mere exercise to a whole therapeutic approach. So this addition has benefited a lot for all the practitioners, in various fields, and also put great emphasis for the need of physical health.

At the time when it was first introduced, Pilates technique was confined to specialized surroundings like studios and Pilates center, but as the benefits of Pilates have outburst at an exponential rate, the facility has now been adopted by various gyms, exercise centers and physiotherapy rooms .The major reason for this diversity in the available spaces for Pilates, can easily be accounted for its highly influential effects and far reaching benefits. Many of the physical instructors are modifying this technique along with their own ways of exercise and physical art. This has made the field of Pilates, a greatly enriched field, in which every new day brings a lot of diversity and new techniques. All over the world people now consider it as more of a therapeutic technique, which is bestowing health and rigor all over the world to millions of people who were hopeless after some ailment or their distorted body type.

Chapter 3:
The Astounding Effects of Pilates

Fitness is the first mandatory for contentment and joy. A common belief about the nature of physical fitness is the accomplishment and continuation of a consistently maintained body with an active mind, which entails the capability of undergoing all tasks with promptness and diligence. To attain the premier success, within the boundaries of one's capacities, in all domains and arenas of life, the preceding significance must be given to get healthier and developed body systems. Once physical rigor is established, it will without human intervention overlay the system towards mental zest and intelligence.

But all this is easy to write and say. Once you start implementing this, you will find a lot many hindrances. Among the supreme challenges is to keep streamlined while being in this challenging world, where everything is hard to achieve. The work pressures, the family demands and the individual needs, all sum up to make the life more messy and challenging. In all this one forgets to think and hover upon his own individual being. Most f the time we think that the last priority we think of, is ourselves. We assume it wrongly that our responsibility is to thrive in all fields of life, leaving behind all necessities of our own health. But in this busy scheduled life, we forget that vigor is foreseeable and remote, despite of all financial resources. Once gone, health needs excessive efforts to be restored.

Physical fitness is both a dilemma and a blessing. It is a kind of state which can never be achieved through heavy investments or by ere thinking. It demands for full exertion and efforts. The results are always twofold. Higher the rate of exertion, definitely higher will be the benefits achieved. But the modern system of human civilization has ruined this need of human being, by engaging it in a number of irrelevant and disastrous tasks, including increased reliance on technology and robotic inventions. Although fiscally one may be mountaineering the ladders of triumph, but the health arena of one's life may fall insolvent. So balancing both sides of the pivot is the key for life, eventually one can be labeled as the real victorious person. If an individual is quite successful in the work life, but he has ruined his health and body, he cannot be labeled as a successful man because he has opted for one, among the two most crucial aspects of life,

Among all these panics and challenges, Pilates has emerged as a major revolutionary step. Among a number of different useful aspects of Pilates, some of them are reflected and discussed below:

For weight loss:

One of the major disasters created by this challenging life is the life routines which ultimately make the human body fatty and overweight. Overweight induces a number of various physical issues which can retain for longer periods, ultimately leading to disasters in human health. Pilates is miraculous for weight loss. The systematic procedures and techniques of Pilates lead towards burning of fat that will assist in making the body slimmed and trimmed, within no time. But the key to triumph is the consistency in the routines and practicing of Pilates. This scheme of body exercise help you monitor your body, modify your breathing patterns, so that all these functions of human body can be changed into an efficient and highly effective body system. Most of the Pilates schemes which are aimed for body weight loss denote the stretching exercises.

For dancers

Pilates is not only for curative purposes, meaning that it is not only a technique for the curative purposes. It is not for all those who have ruined their body postures and shape, it can also help a lot many who are involved in a number of stretching professions or other activities which involve excessive physical outputs. Among these professionals, one of the largest groups involves dancers. Dancers are therapists who use their body language to convey their art. They cannot afford even a minimum sort of body disturbances. Moreover, a number of Pilate's techniques involve the postures which ultimately lead to highly flexible body organs, so it aid in using the body more effectively by the dancers. Various dancers have reported that they have experienced a wide appreciation because of changed body reflexive due to Pilates.

During pregnancy

Many women think that they are cannot exert much physical efforts if they have got pregnant. Pregnancy does not denote physical statistic. It must be accompanied with healthy routines and living patterns. Pilates is a distinctive workout scheme which can pose a number of techniques for pregnant ladies, which will not only lend a hand to them for retaining their body shapes but will also aid in progressive development of the baby's body. Although pregnancy needs excessive monitoring for body, yet it does not demand that all the physical activity must be stopped immediately after getting the good news. The whole period of pregnancy must be engaged in a way that it becomes productive for the health and physique, not a burden. Pilates introduces some basic regimes of body and leg movement for all ladies who are having these issues and help them cater their pregnancy in a better way. If the women start it form the initial stage to last stage she will definitely enjoy an overwhelmingly secure and sound pregnancy without any complications.

For belly fat

Some specific issues addressed by Pilates also include the belly fat issues. Any excessive fat deposit or lipoid-deposit is easily manageable by some modified techniques of Pilates, which help in calorie burning and fat dissolution. Many of the thinkers hold the analysis that belly fat reduction demands for a consistent approach towards following a regular scheme. Belly fat reduction is considered as one of the major challenges as well as a hindrance towards slim and trim body. Many of the Pilates techniques have been specially modified, to help a large number of people, who are facing a downturn in their body. The reason for this downturn is the increased fat on their belly. It also hits the body and the personality charisma. No one likes to be recognized by a loose tummy. So Pilates can help everyone start an energetic and charismatic life by trimming the belly and making all the muscles healthy strong and still attractive.

For back pain

One of the key reasons for back ache is the distorted body postures. These postures are usually induced by unhealthy sitting postures and uncomfortable sitting plan. Moreover back pain can be because of higher tendency towards obesity and the tendency of being overweight. All these basic reasons can contribute towards the highly painful condition of back ache. Pilates is aimed at not only curing back ache nut also preventing it in all those, who have not encountered it. The stretching exercises and the postures introduced by Pilates help in strengthen of spinal cord and the vertebrae so that it can maintain the back strength and avoid all the reasons effectively. Back ache has been reported to be one of the major reasons of distorted body shapes, so eradicating it form the basic level is highly crucial.

For abs

Another misconception about Pilate's method is that it is only a way of correcting the posture, body movements and breathing patterns. Many people are devoid of the information that Pilates is also for all those who want to build up a muscular body. Abs building is another miracle of Pilate's scheme of exercise. Although the scheme and pattern of exercise will be quite transformed for abs building, yet Pilates is not devoid of these kinds of techniques which are helpful for body builders and all those who are interested in muscle formation. Many people have been successful in building and sustain their abs because they have consistently followed Pilate's scheme.

Chapter 4:
Starting With Pilates

Pilates or as proposed by its inventor, Contrology is an absolute synchronization and dexterity of soul, mind and body. In the course of learning and practicing Pilates the practitioners first decisively obtain an efficient control over all the body movements and functions and this control and management is then utilized to acquire the synchronization of soul and subconscious activities. When all the different domains of the body and soul are following the same synchronization and harmony, the eventual result will be the healthy and peaceful body.

But all this harmonization and management requires consistency and the sense of determination so that repetitive Pilates practicing can lead you to achieve your desired goals.

Pilates is the most renowned and effective technique for correcting imbalanced body postures, developing body health, enhancing the spirits and restoring the physical vivacity. These characteristics are basically inbuilt in the human body, when the humans are in the early age of infancy, when soul and body directions are same, coherent and efficient. But this purity and synchronization is soon lost when the infant steadily moves toward maturity and start facing the harsh and cruel realities of life. During this course of challenging battle with the realities of life, the first thing that gets hurt is the physical attire of the human body. The aftermaths can be experiential in the shape of fatigued eyes, callous crows' feet, spun out shoulders and indistinct postures. Many people consider it to be the aftermaths of growing age but this is not true because growing age does not connotes bad health. All we need is to restore the vitality and rigor of our body and taking care of our soul and busy as some precious treasure, upon which the whole essence of our success relies. Pilates is among some techniques which help you revitalize your body muscles and strengths.

Principles of Pilates:

Although we can have been discussing what the field of Pilates technique for body stability has become such a diverse field that different sort of modifications, alterations and additions have made it more useful technique, yet some basics of Pilates involves the core themes of principles of this techniques.

- **Concentration**

The core is to concentrate. Many of you may ask that when we are overwhelmed with so much of work pressures and deadlines that getting in the stream of focus is quite near to impossible. So Pilate's techniques help you to develop and craft the ability to concentrate. Concentration is vital because Pilate's scheme of exercise is aimed at making the individual relieved form the worries and pressures, so by developing concentration these exercises can easily let the practitioner get away from the worries and concentration the workout. The actual results of this technique are also visible when the stage of concentration becomes achievable.

- **Control**

Control denotes the power of managing the body movements, muscular strengths and body patterns. Although these principles are the successive steps of Pilate's technique, yet they are highly interrelated. Concentration and excess of focus will eventually pave your way towards body control and management. Many of you may ponder upon the need for control. The basic theme of Pilates is to let everyone enjoy the manageability if ones, body movements and postures, so Pilates will help you learn this.

- **Centering**

In Pilates scheme of exercise the focus on some initial point of reference or centering position. Most if the viewpoints regarding the center have made the central abdominal region as the main focus of the body movements and the point of management. Hence the entire scheme of abdominal muscles and the limbs are highly focused and maintained to serve as the center of strength and rigor.

- **Flow of movement**

Once the control over the body is achieved than the trainers usually advice to start practicing the management of movements and dynamic systems of the body. The limbs are highly focused, so that the movements are according to the standards of efficient body which can correct the body postures and tart paving the way to vitalized body. Once the body movements are managed they will become the part of human routines and working style so that physical stress cannot destroy the human health.

- **Precision**

Accuracy is the critical and crucial factor. The entire the activities and posters experienced in that scheme of study are designed with zero error precision, as human body is also prone to is management. Although human body denotes strength and rigor yet it can be fragile if exposed to mismanaged body postures and movements. So the instructors of Pilates usually take care of this aspect and design every exercise according individual inclinations and abilities. A slight ignorance from the individual needs of the human body can drastically destroy the precision of the exercise and the fruitful results of the exercise can never be accounted. Precision looks very irrelevant to common man as far as the physical output is considered, yet it lies as the main foundation of Pilates.

- **Breathing**

Apart from body movements the basics of human body control is the pattern of breathing. One trivial amendment and improvement in breathing patterns and techniques can help the human body enjoy the maximum of power and vitality. Pilate's instructor helps individuals use this function of human body as the source of power. Individuals are taught t breath with efficient styles and using different routes, which also varies according to individual objectives. Many of the latent faulty working and diseases of the human body can easily be eradicated if the breathing is considered not only as the function of human body but also strength for gaining the ultimate vitality and health.

- **Power house**

Another distinctive characteristic of this scheme of physical exercise and output is the focus on the power house with reference to the human body as a system harmonized organs. As per the philosophy of Pilates the power house resides within the centre of human body. So all the basic principles focused above ultimately lead to the strengthening of this power house.

Chapter 5:
Comparative analysis- Pilates vs. Yoga

Choosing and diagnosing the right therapy for your body is no less than a challenge. This entails both the physical as well mental therapies. Having so much advancement in every field of medicine as well as the physical sciences, all of us are surrounded by plenty of choices and options. But this excessiveness is also enhancing the confusions as well as misinterpretations. People get whirled by these options because there raises a long held debate on all types of options and alternatives. Every single method has millions of followers along with same number of opponents, who are making the debates more long and complicate. Many groups fallaciously deem that Pilates is like other forms of exercises, only with a changed name. But whatever form of exercise you are using you should have an in depth understanding regarding the purpose, possible alternatives and the core theme for each type of exercise. The major form of exercise with which Pilates is mostly mixed or assorted, is Yoga. One cannot affirm or rule out that Pilates scheme is more effective than Yoga or vice versa but the underlying basics is that one should know how to differentiate between the two and how to choose the method appropriate for the particular needed of the body.

Pilates vs. Yoga

- Picking and deciding between these two techniques is quite crucial and critical because it demands for a systematic analysis and thoughtful reasoning.

- For the supporters of yoga or Pilates, their particular situate of calisthenics is the best preference presented. And they are rather defensible in the sense that they choose the respective set if exercise for attainment of their particular goals and agendas.

- As far as Yoga is concerned the core of this scheme is focus on breathing so that the human movements and functions get tuned with the rhythm and harmony of breathing patterns. Moreover the technique is also considered as a technique of soul. Yogis usually connote that the human soul and body must be moving and struggling in one single direction.

- On the other hand Pilates is a scheme with the central attention towards body movements and postures. Although breathing is a major section for the hub of Pilates, practitioner, yet it entails supremacy to be related with central muscles of human body.

- As far as the historical perspectives are concerned, Pilates can be regarded as a set of contemporary techniques, developed in the modern era of progress and development. Whereas Yoga connotes a technique which has a long reported history of even two or more centuries back. so as far as the alterations is concerned Pilates has been subjected t little alterations as compared to Yoga, which after passing from generation to generation has merged with a number of different cultural aspects and demographic inclinations.

- As largely followed rule of thumb if the goal is to get solid muscular abdominal region than people chose Pilates as the most appropriate way, but for concentration and focus achievements, Yoga is the largely focused technique.

- Pilates is based on a number of finely tuned apparatus and movement machines for delivering the accurate and required results according to the customized and desired goals of very individual. Whereas Yoga can be practiced without any automation kit, definite breathing designs are involved and focused in yoga.

Chapter 6:
Precautionary Measures and
Concluding Remarks

A major contribution and consequence of Pilates is the intense help in gaining the eventual control and charge of the body so that nothing can affect the human body. But any people believe that Pilates is not effective only because they had been unable to get to the real way of practicing and extracting the techniques of Pilates. But on the other side of the picture, Pilates has emerged as a revolutionary aid for many others who have lived upon this technique for years and years. The distinctive method is a diverse set of ideas governing and maintaining human body and soul in an unparallel way.

Some may label it unsuccessful because their mind has a permanent impression of fruitless exercises because of some previous bad experience. Again the root cause lies in implementing the method accurately. Pilates also affects the brain parts, many people have reported that the activity of brain cells is largely triggered by this distinguishing method of body flow and movement, so that one is able to get an eventual control and concern towards all the functions of human body and mind.

In the end we will suggest all those who have looked upon this book that they should start focusing on their strengths and weaknesses. Physical health is not something which can be put down in ignore list, rather it should be in the priority list so that one s able to extract the maximum benefit out of this world and its blessings.

Pilates is no doubt a challenging technique if you want to get full benefits of it with long-lasting and wider benefits. But once you get on the track nothing is impossible. Start working on extracting the methods of getting mastery over this technique. Some initial faults in your method of implementation may not be the indicators of failure of this method. It is not also a hit and trial method in which you can make deletions and additions with your own prescriptions. It is a long held rule of exercise and physical output that needs to be implemented in its true spirits.

The attainment and gratification of physical rigor, mental tranquil and divine serenity is incalculably precious to their individuals if someone gets this miraculous combination, in today's world of fuss and messed up routines. However, it is not the matter of gaining these blessings; the real task is to maintain this exclusive combination of effectiveness from human body to human soul and subconscious. One simple way is to start practicing Pilates from today and the eventual results will be overwhelming for all of us, in terms of healthier and more effective societies. Together we can bring the cumulative development and vitality.

Conclusion

Thank you again for downloading this book!

I hope this book was able to help you to start living your life as you should.

The next step is to apply what you've learned on a daily basis.

Finally, if you enjoyed this book, please take the time to share your thoughts and post a review on Amazon. It'd be greatly appreciated!

Thank you and good luck!